ALIGNING YOURSELF
WITH GOD

The Sin Crouching At Your Door

Crystal A. Hood

i

DEDICATION

This book is dedicated to my Lord and Savior Jesus Christ.
He saw the needs of my heart then blessed me with a husband and children who are
beyond amazing

ABRAHAM'S FAITH
Romans 4:1-3;4: 18-25

What then shall we say that Abraham, our forefather, has discovered?

If Abraham was indeed justified by works, he had something to boast about, but not before God.

For what does the Scripture say? "Abraham believed God, and it was credited to him as righteousness."

Against all hope, Abraham in hope believed and so became the father of many nations, just as he had been told, "So shall your offspring be."

Without weakening in his faith, he acknowledged the decrepitness of his body (since he was about a hundred years old) and the lifelessness of Sarah's womb.

Yet he did not waver through disbelief in the promise of God, but was strengthened in his faith and gave glory to God, being fully persuaded that God was able to do what He had promised. That is why "it was credited to him as righteousness."

Now the words "it was credited to him" were written not only for Abraham, but also for us, to whom righteousness will be credited—for us who believe in Him who raised Jesus our Lord from the dead. He was delivered over to death for our trespasses and was raised to life for our justification.

CONTENTS

PREFACE

Praise God! Praise God! Praise God!

Since 2010 I have had the privilege of writing for the magazine "The Encourager" which is published quarterly by Columbia Community Church in Columbia Maryland. During this time the Holy Spirit has guided me
through a variety of spiritual moments and biblical insights.

I believe God has been sharing a consistent message in the articles that He has had me write; that message is the importance of aligning our lives to His will. I have taken those articles and have broken them into a series of small books.

 My goals in creating these books are to provide a resource for biblical steps we can take to put ourselves in a position to hear God, connect to Him and continue toward Him. Also, to give honor to God and for it to be used as a venue in which the Holy Spirit can teach, convict, encourage and transform us and our families to His will.

This book is the third book in the series Aligning Yourself with God. It has five main topics. Each section has a reflection page and a list of scriptures connected to the topic.

At the end of the book there is a "Steps to Align with God" area. It is a resource to help direct you in prayer, reflection, action and thanks toward God.

I pray this book is a blessing and a useful tool in which the Holy Spirit may challenge and guide you as you strive toward God and aligning your life toward His will

INTRODUCTION

The Bible tells of a situation in which a father brought his son to Jesus' disciples. The disciples were unable to help him. When Jesus came upon the scene the father presented his problem to Jesus.

"Teacher, I brought You my son, who has a spirit that makes him mute. Whenever it seizes him, it throws him to the ground. He foams at the mouth, gnashes his teeth, and becomes rigid. I asked Your disciples to drive it out, but they were unable."

"O unbelieving generation!" Jesus replied. "How long must I remain with you? How long must I put up with you? Bring the boy to Me."

So they brought him and seeing Jesus, the spirit immediately threw the boy into a convulsion. He fell to the ground and rolled around, foaming at the mouth.

Jesus asked the boy's father, "How long has this been with him?"

"From childhood," he said. "It often throws him into the fire or into the water, trying to kill him. But if You can do anything, have compassion on us and help us."

"If You can?" echoed Jesus. "All things are possible to him who believes!" Mark 9:17-23

Jesus' heart aches for them. He knows that He will not be with this generation much longer and their unbelief is hindering them from receiving from God.

The man responds in a surrendered prayer

Immediately the boy's father cried out, "I do believe; help my unbelief!" Mark 9:24

This father's heartfelt admission is simply a request to have his faith fortified. It is one that we have all needed at some point in our life.

Our ability to believe God is essential to our relationship with Him. It is the key to our connection to God and the power of God in our life.

And without faith it is impossible to please God, because anyone who approaches Him must believe that He exists and that He rewards those who earnestly seek Him. Hebrews 11:6

Unbelief is a sin. Most people understand sin to mean wrong things that they do against God. When Moses led God's people through the desert, their worst sin was the wrong attitude of their hearts (Hebrews 3:8). This particular sin is called unbelief which is synonymous with a lack of faith.

We do not believe God is who He says He is or we do not believe He will do what He says He will do.

Another situation concerning faith is recorded in the Old Testament of the Bible. It relays a conversation that God had with Cain, the son of Adam and Eve. Cain's offering to God had been rejected by Him. God then reached out to Cain about what happened.

"And the LORD said to Cain, "Why are you so angry? And why do you look annoyed? If you do well [believing Me and doing what is acceptable and pleasing to Me], will you not be accepted? And if you do not do well [but ignore My instruction], sin crouches at your door; its desire is for you [to overpower you], but you must master it." Genesis 4:6-7 (Amplified Bible).

In both of these events, the people involved are struggling. They are having difficulty because there are things unseen that are influencing their faith. What is unseen is the existence of sin and Satan.

Crouching is a great adjective to describe both sin and Satan. By definition it means to adopt a position in a way that avoids detection; to creep up on us in a way that we don't notice.

That is the essence of sin and the character of Satan. Both are key instruments in corrupting our ability to believe God and align ourselves with Him.

God does not desire for us to be blind to these influences. He provides the Holy Spirit and His Word, the Bible, as the source for our eyes to be open.

In this book, we will seek both as a means for us to see the sin crouching at our door.

Sin and Satan crouch at our door and try to overpower us, but Jesus stands and knocks at our door. He asks to come in.

It is up to us to invite Him in.

I STAND AT THE DOOR AND KNOCK
Revelation 3:20-22

Jesus stated, Behold, I stand at the door and knock.

If anyone hears My voice and opens the door,

I will come in and dine with him, and he with Me.

To the one who overcomes,

I will grant the right to sit with Me on My throne,

just as I overcame and sat down with My Father on His throne.

He who has an ear, let him hear what the Spirit says to the churches."

SECTION 1

THE IMAGE AND LIKENESS OF THE HOLY TRINITY

In the beginning God created the heavens and the earth.

Genesis 1:1

THE IMAGE AND LIKENESS OF THE HOLY TRINITY

O n the sixth day, God created Adam and Eve in the image and likeness of the Holy Trinity (Genesis 1:26-36). Being in the image and likeness of the Holy Trinity refers to the spiritual nature of Adam and Eve.

They held a unique physical and spiritual connection to God and each other (Genesis 2:15-25). They walked and talked with God face to face. Adam acknowledged and accepted Eve as the flesh of his flesh and bone of his bone.

When God created Adam he told him not to eat of the tree of knowledge of good and evil.

"And the LORD God commanded him, "You may eat freely from every tree of the garden, but you must not eat from the tree of the knowledge of good and evil; for in the day that you eat of it, you will surely die." Genesis 2:16

Their problems began when Eve was deceived by the serpent and ate of the tree. Then Eve gave Adam the fruit. He chose to disobey God and ate. In that instance, everything changed for them. They no longer had the spiritual nature of God. They now had the sinful nature of Satan.

What is sin? Sin is not just the actions we commit or omit; it is the destruction and the decay of everything that God created perfect and good. It is the tacit admission that we know better than God what is best for us.

Sin, in essence, is agreeing with Satan; that his way is better than God's ways. It is, like Satan, believing that we are equal or better than God.

When Adam ate of the fruit he directly disobeyed God's command. His act was different from Eve's. Eve was deceived into disobeying God.

The Spirit tells us, *"Anyone, then, who knows the right thing to do, yet fails to do it, is guilty of sin."* James 4:17

God's Word also states,
The one who practices sin [separating himself from God, and offending Him by acts of disobedience, indifference, or rebellion] is of the devil [and takes his inner character and moral values from him, not God]; 1 John 3:8 (Amplified Bible)

What do these events mean to us?

As descendants of Adam, we inherited the same sinful nature within us.

This is the book of the generations of Adam. In the day that God created man, He made him in His own likeness. Male and female He created them, and He blessed them. And in the day they were created, He called them "man."

When Adam was 130 years old, he had a son in his own likeness, after his own image; Genesis 5:1-3

Therefore, just as sin entered the world through one man, and death through sin, so also death was passed on to all men, because all sinned. Romans 5:12

How did sin change us and the earth?

After Adam and Eve ate from the tree of knowledge of good and evil their eyes were instantly opened and they knew that they were naked. They quickly covered themselves with leaves. Then they heard God coming and they hid. Genesis 3:7-8.

At this moment two things happened that directly correlate to sin. Shame and Fear now exist within man. Due to sin they now feared God and felt shame in being bare before Him. They now desired to hide from Him and held the mistaken belief that they could hide from Him.

Previously, Adam and Eve had no problem being naked in the presence of God. Naked in this sense is both physical and spiritual. They were created in the image and likeness of the Holy Trinity. They shared the same Spirit of unity as the Holy Trinity.

Prior to them eating the fruit, having companionship with the creator of everything did not cause fear or shame. They were bare and open before Him. They had not attempted to hide anything from God. They continually experienced a spiritual connection to God and daily experienced the physical presence of God. It is because of the sin in them, that they now responded to God differently. Sin and the way they responded to God are now imbedded in all of mankind.

When God comes to them He first called out to Adam and said, "Where are you?" He then asks Eve, "What have you done?" He knew the answer to these questions.

God is omniscient. He does not ask us questions because He is lacking knowledge. He asks us questions so we can see what is going on within us.

The relationship Adam and Eve had with Him changed. They needed to see that it changed, confess what they had done and seek His forgiveness. Also, their relationship with each other changed.

From the beginning, God created a special bond between Adam and his wife. They were one. Once Adam ate and broke the commandment of God the unity between man and woman became twisted.

Adam tells God, *"I heard Your voice in the garden,"* he replied, *"and I was afraid because I was naked; so I hid myself."*

"Who told you that you were naked?" asked the LORD God. "Have you eaten from the tree of which I commanded you not to eat?"

And the man answered, "The woman whom You gave me, she gave me fruit from the tree, and I ate it." Genesis 3:10-12

Adam did not acknowledge his responsibility or the fact that he broke the commandment that had been given directly to him. He now feels shame, is fearful of God, deflects responsibility, and scorns the blessing of the wife that God had given him. Adam's mind has changed. His way of thinking has changed.

God then addresses Eve. She states that she was deceived by the serpent, which is true, he did entice her. During Eve's conversation with Satan, her perspective shifted away from who God said she was and shifted toward who Satan said she should be.

She was Adam's helpmate. Her role was to be beside him in fulfilling the responsibilities and command that God gave him. When she ate the fruit and gave Adam the fruit she stepped out of the role that God gave her. She was not helping Adam to keep his responsibilities and the command of God.

God then proceeds to outline for them the consequence of their sin. Genesis 3:16-20. These are not God's punishments upon them. Adam was given dominion and authority over everything. When Adam ate from the fruit he was being obedient to Satan not to God. He transferred those rights to Satan. Adam's sin, like a disease, infected everything.

God said to the woman that her pain during childbirth would increase. She will also desire her husband and that he would rule over her.

Having intense pain during childbirth altered from what God had originally established. Also, the oneness that she and Adam easily experienced before eating the fruit was replaced with contention, discord, and opposition. Men are going to try to dominate women and women are going to fight against men.

God said to Adam, *"Because you have listened to the voice of your wife and have eaten from the tree of which I commanded you not to eat, cursed is the ground because of you;* Genesis 3:17

God is letting him know that life is about to be difficult. His disobedience not only impacted him spiritually, but it changed the earth as well. Before he sinned, caring for the garden was not difficult. The ground was fertile. They had plenty of food to eat. They did not need clothing or shelter.

God tells him that *"through toil you will eat of it all the days of your life. Both thorns and thistles it will yield for you, and you will eat the plants of the field. By the sweat of your brow you will eat your bread, until you return to the ground—because out of it were you taken. For dust you are, and to dust you shall return."* Genesis 3:17-19

Finally, God lets Adam know that because of his disobedience life has limits. He will labor all of his life. Then he will eventually die and return to dust.

Our sinful nature makes it difficult for us to fathom the initial experience Adam and Eve had with God. This is because we no longer have the mind of God to see as He sees. Our belief in the first three chapters of Genesis is the foundation of our faith. It opens our eyes to the:

beginning of life

creation of male and female

union of one male and one female in marriage

spiritual unity between God and mankind

influence of Satan

origin of sin in mankind,

 impact of sin on mankind and the earth.

The Bible is based precept upon precept (Isaiah 28:10). A precept is a principle or guideline. Understanding one precept helps to understand the next one. Comprehending and understanding one piece of biblical truth that God has revealed helps us to understand another biblical truth. These Biblical truths are consistent and connect from Genesis to Revelations.

When building our faith by accepting one precept at a time ensures that we are heading in the right direction. Paul stated that we see dimly as though looking through a mirror. We will not fully grasp everything until we are in heaven (1 Corinthians 13:12). It is because of this that we walk not by sight but by faith (2 Corinthians 5:7).

Our foundation of faith established on Genesis 1-3 is the groundwork toward us understanding the life we now experience.

Through these Biblical truths, we are able to see how God originally established things. We start to see the global impact sin had on us and the world. It lets us know how we are on the earth and with each other are due to sin.

When we believe in what happened to Adam and Eve it helps us toward gaining insight into the dramatic separation we experienced from God; we are no longer created in His image but are born in sin and our sinful nature continues to separate us from Him.

Also, when we believe in what transpired in the beginning, we start to see that our sinful nature infects (like a disease) on our ability to believe God. It holds us captive to the influence of Satan and his way of thinking.

Finally, as we see the overall impact of our sinful nature our eyes are open to the fact that we can never bridge the gap between us and God.

No matter how good we try to be, we still have a sinful nature and can never be in the presence of God. We need a savior to bridge that gap and restore our relationship and connection to God (Romans 7:21-25)

The Son of God appeared for this purpose, to destroy the works of the devil. 1John 3:8 (Amplified Bible)

God is.....

Holy – God's perfection of character and without flaw and without sin but with complete goodness, justice, mercy, love, etc.

Isaiah 6:3
And they were calling out to one another: "Holy, holy, holy is the LORD of Hosts;
all the earth is full of His glory."

Leviticus 19:2
"Speak to the whole congregation of Israel and tell them: Be holy because I, the LORD your God, am holy.

Spirit - God exists completely and sufficiently as an immaterial being--without physical characteristics.

John 4:24
God is Spirit, and His worshipers must worship Him in spirit and in truth."

Luke 24:39
Look at My hands and My feet. It is I Myself. Touch Me and see—for a spirit does not have flesh and bones, as you see I have."

Immutable – God's nature does not change in any way. His essence has always been and will always be exactly the same.

Malachi 3:6
"Because I, the LORD, do not change

Hebrews 13:8
Jesus Christ is the same yesterday and today and forever.

Infinite – God is without measure or limit in reach or continuation. There are no constraints upon him from outside of himself that would restrict him in his reach or continuation. He is **self – existent**- God is not dependent upon anything else for his existence. He is the infinite Being who has always existed. He is **self-sufficient** - God needs nothing outside of himself to maintain his existence; therefore, he does not need us to fill a void

Psalm 90:2
Before the mountains were born or You brought forth the earth and the world, from everlasting to everlasting You are God.

Isaiah 40:28
Do you not know? Have you not heard? The LORD is the everlasting God, the Creator of the ends of the earth. He will not grow tired or weary; His understanding is beyond searching out.

Psalm 93:2
Your throne was established long ago; You are from all eternity.

Revelation 1:8
"I am the Alpha and the Omega," says the Lord God, who is and was and is to come—the Almighty.

Omnipotent -God is capable of performing anything he desires. He is **sovereign -** God is the Supreme Being who answers to no one and who has the absolute right to do with his creation as he desires.

Psalm 33:9
For He spoke, and it came to be; He commanded, and it stood firm.

Isaiah 46:10

I declare the end from the beginning, and ancient times from what is still to come. I say, 'My purpose will stand, and all My good pleasure I will accomplish.'

Omnipresent - God is in all places and in all dimensions simultaneously. Nothing in the universe exists outside the presence of God. He is **transcendent** - God's transcendence is the product of the relationship between God's essence and creation. God transcends space and time in that he is not dependent on them nor affected by them.

Psalm 139:7-12

Where can I go to escape Your Spirit? Where can I flee from Your presence?

If I ascend to the heavens, You are there; if I make my bed in Sheol, You are there.

If I rise on the wings of the dawn, if I settle by the farthest sea, even there Your hand will guide me; Your right hand will hold me fast.

If I say, "Surely the darkness will hide me, and the light become night around me"— even the darkness is not dark to You, but the night shines like the day, for darkness is as light to You.

Jeremiah 23:23-24

"Am I only a God nearby," declares the LORD, "and not a God far away?" "Can a man hide in secret places where I cannot see him?" declares the LORD. "Do I not fill the heavens and the earth?" declares the LORD.

Omniscient - God has perfect, complete knowledge. He never learns, nor does he forget. He knows all things that exist and all things that could have existed. God has all knowledge, understanding, and wisdom.

Romans 16:27

to the only wise God be glory forever through Jesus Christ! Amen.

Hebrews 4:13

Nothing in all creation is hidden from God's sight; everything is uncovered and exposed before the eyes of Him to whom we must give account.

1 John 3:20

If our hearts condemn us, God is greater than our hearts, and He knows all things.

Unique - God alone is God. There is no one like him. He is completely "other" than all things that exist

Isaiah 44:6-7

Thus says the LORD, the King and Redeemer of Israel, the LORD of Hosts: "I am the first and I am the last, and there is no God but Me.

Who then is like Me? Let him say so! Let him declare his case before Me, since I established an ancient people. Let him foretell the things to come, and what is to take place.

Scriptures: Sin

God and Sin

Habakkuk 1:13 NASB
Your eyes are too pure to approve evil, And You can not look on wickedness with favor.

Isaiah 64:5
You welcome those who gladly do right, who remember Your ways. Surely You were angry, for we sinned. How can we be saved if we remain in our sins?

Jeremiah 2:22
Although you wash with lye and use an abundance of soap, the stain of your guilt is still before Me,"

James 1:13
When tempted, no one should say, "God is tempting me." For God cannot be tempted by evil, nor does He tempt anyone.

2 Chronicles 7:14
and My people who are called by My name humble themselves and pray and seek My face and turn from their wicked ways then I will hear from heaven, forgive their sin, and heal their land. (God)

1 John 1:5
And this is the message we have heard from Him and announce to you: God is light, and in Him there is no darkness at all.

Isaiah 59:1-3
Surely the arm of the LORD is not too short to save, nor His ear too dull to hear. But your iniquities have built barriers between you and your God, and your sins have hidden His face from you, so that He does not hear.

Isaiah 1:15

When you spread out your hands in prayer,
I will hide My eyes from you; even though you multiply your
prayers, I will not listen. Your hands are covered with blood.

Us and Sin

Romans 3:23
for all have sinned and fall short of the glory of God,

James 4:17-21
Anyone, then, who knows the right thing to do, yet fails to do it, is guilty of sin.

Isaiah 6:5 NASB
Then I said, "Woe is me, for I am ruined! Because I am a man of unclean lips, And I live among a people of unclean lips; For my eyes have seen the King, the LORD of hosts."

Romans 6:16
Do you not know that when you offer yourselves as obedient slaves, you are slaves to the one you obey, whether you are slaves to sin leading to death, or to obedience leading to righteousness?

James 1:13
But each one is tempted when by his own evil desires he is lured away and enticed, Then after desire has conceived, it gives birth to sin; and sin, when it is full-grown, gives birth to death.

Romans 5:12-14
Therefore, just as sin entered the world through one man, and death through sin, so also death was passed on to all men, because all sinned

John 8:34
Jesus replied, "Truly, truly, I tell you, everyone who sins is a slave to sin.

Proverbs 5:22
The iniquities of a wicked man entrap him; the cords of his sin entangle him.

Isaiah 64:6
Each of us has become like something unclean, and all our righteous acts are like filthy rags; we all wither like a leaf, and our iniquities carry us away like the wind.

Matthew 15:18-19

But the things that come out of the mouth come from the heart, and these things defile a man. For out of the heart come evil thoughts, murder, adultery, sexual immorality, theft, false testimony, and slander.

Romans 1:21

For although they knew God, they neither glorified Him as God nor gave thanks to Him, but they became futile in their thinking and darkened in their foolish hearts.

Proverbs 14:34

Righteousness exalts a nation, but sin is a disgrace to any people.

The Earth and Sin

Leviticus 18:25
Even the land has become defiled, so I am punishing it for its sin, and the land will vomit out its inhabitants.

Romans 8:20-22
For the creation was subjected to futility, not by its own will, but because of the One who subjected it, in hope that the creation itself will be set free from its bondage to decay and brought into the glorious freedom of the children of God.

We know that the whole creation has been groaning together in the pains of childbirth until the present time.

Genesis 4:10-12
"What have you done?" replied the LORD. "The voice of your brother's blood cries out to Me from the ground.

Now you are cursed and banished from the ground, which has opened its mouth to receive your brother's blood from your hand.

When you till the ground, it will no longer yield its produce to you. You will be a fugitive and a wanderer on the earth."

Numbers 35:33
Do not pollute the land where you live, for bloodshed pollutes the land,

Isaiah 24:4-6
The earth mourns and withers; the world languishes and fades; the exalted of the earth waste away.

The earth is defiled by its people; they have transgressed the laws; they have overstepped the decrees and broken the everlasting covenant.

Therefore a curse has consumed the earth, and its inhabitants must bear the guilt; the earth's dwellers have been burned, and only a few survive.

Take Time to Pray, Reflect, and Write

For the word of God is living and active. Sharper than any double-edged sword, it **pierces** *even to dividing soul and spirit, joints and marrow. It judges the thoughts and intentions of the heart.*

Nothing in all creation is hidden from God's sight; everything is uncovered and exposed before the eyes of Him to whom we must give account. Hebrews 4:12-13

Pray about what you have read.

Reflect on the topic and scriptures provided in the section

Write down your reflections from what you read:

- How did God's Word touch your spirit from this topic?

- In what areas did the Holy Spirit affirm God's Word in your heart?

- Did you receive a revelation from what you read? If so what?

- Is God asking you a question?

SECTION 2

A SIMPLE ACT

For God did not send His Son into the world to condemn the world, but to save the world through Him.

John 3:17

ALIVE IN CHRIST
Romans 8:1-4

Therefore, there is now no condemnation for those who are in Christ Jesus.

For in Christ Jesus the law of the

Spirit of life has set you free from the law of sin and death.

For what the law was powerless to do in that it was weakened by the flesh,

God did by sending His own Son in the likeness of sinful man, as an offering for sin.

He thus condemned sin in the flesh,

so that the righteous standard of the law might be fulfilled in us,

WHO DO NOT WALK ACCORDING TO THE FLESH BUT ACCORDING TO THE SPIRIT.

A SIMPLE ACT

I remember when I was twelve years old I went to a Salvation Army summer camp. On Sunday we had a service. At the end of the service, the minister asked if anyone wanted to receive Jesus as savior. I practically ran from my seat.

I left everyone that was a part of my friendship group. I remember thinking, "If this is all it takes to get to Jesus and heaven, I'm in." That young simple-minded childlike belief is what Jesus spoke about.

Then the little children were brought to Jesus for Him to place His hands on them and pray for them. And the disciples rebuked those who brought them. But Jesus said, "Let the little children come to Me, and do not hinder them! For the kingdom of heaven belongs to such as these."
Matthew 19:13-14

As adults, we make things more complicated than they are. We put stipulations on how we should come to Christ, whether we are worthy to come and a list of pre-requisites to be completed prior to coming to Jesus.

We don't fully understand the ugliness of sin before a Holy God. It's putrid. We are born with that filth in us. When God asked Eve "What have you done?" There is a magnitude to that question. There is a depth to the seriousness of what transpired. The problem that now existed because of what happened is monumental.

Sin is like having fresh feces constantly on you that you can't get off. You can spray air freshener and deodorizer on yourself and around you. At times, the smell is decreased, but never really gone and you are still covered in excrement. There is nothing of man pure enough or powerful enough to cover the filth.

God shows through the laws of the Old Testament the extent required for the stench of our sin to be less offensive to Him.

Since Adam, sin has dwelt within us. There is an internal battle within us between wanting to follow God and wanting to give in to our sinful nature. Paul beautifully described this dilemma.

So this is the principle I have discovered: When I want to do good, evil is right there with me. For in my inner being I delight in God's law.

But I see another law at work in my body, warring against the law of my mind and holding me captive to the law of sin that dwells within me. What a wretched man I am! Who will rescue me from this body of death? Thanks be to God, through Jesus Christ our Lord! Romans 7:21-25

God loves us. What happened in the Garden of Eden separated us from Him. His desire is for us to be reconnected to Him. Jesus is that connector He sent Jesus to be the covering for our sin. Jesus is God and man. He was born of a virgin.

"How can this be," Mary asked the angel, "since I am a virgin?"

The angel replied, "The Holy Spirit will come upon you, and the power of the Most High will overshadow you. So the Holy One to be born will be called the Son of God. Luke 1:34-35

Jesus has the purity and power of God through the Holy Spirit. He was born of a woman and lived on Earth. He knew love, pain, suffering, hunger, heartache, rejection and more.

Through Jesus' life, we see the love of God and God's glory in its fullness. We see God displayed in a way that He foretold about through the prophets of the Old Testament.

Jesus is the one sacrifice able to cleanse us of the filth of sin. He was the only one able to take on all of the sewage of mankind and become that one sacrifice for all eternity.

For God so loved the world that He gave His one and only Son, that everyone who believes in Him shall not perish but have eternal life. For God did not send His Son into the world to condemn the world, but to save the world through Him. John 3:16-17

Condemned means: to endure painful punishment, especially death; being found guilty.

Again, there is no sacrifice that we can do or make that will cleanse us of the filth of sin. We can't work out of it, buy our way out of it or die our way out of it. We can't pray enough, be good enough, or be holy enough to cleanse us from sin.

Whoever believes in Him is not condemned, but whoever does not believe has already been condemned, because he has not believed in the name of God's one and only Son John 3:17-18

God says we are already condemned. He sent Jesus to deliver us from His coming judgment. This is the proof of God's love, for while we were still sinners - while we were disobedient, rebellious, idolaters, dismissive and repudiative (rejecting emphatically) - Christ died for us (Romans 5:6-8). All we have to do is believe in His Word.

Three days after Jesus died He was raised from the

dead. This displayed the power and glory of God over sin and death.

Sin is death. It kills us physically and spiritually. It corrupts and destroys. Jesus was the sacrifice for our sin and He is the power for us over sin. Like Paul stated we still have a sin nature, but we now have Jesus.

But what does it say? "The word is near you; it is in your mouth and in your heart," that is, the word of faith we are proclaiming: that if you confess with your mouth, "Jesus is Lord," and believe in your heart that God raised Him from the dead, you will be saved.

For with your heart you believe and are justified, and with your mouth you confess and are saved. Romans 10:8-10

When I went forward to ask Jesus to come into my heart I knew within me that I was unworthy. I knew my internal thoughts and mind. I also desired to be near Jesus. Once I made my confession of faith I was different. I felt free. It was that simple.

This is what being born again is all about. It is one of the most amazing and powerful miracles from God. It is a simple and necessary action in order for us to enter the kingdom of God (John 3:3).

Through Jesus, we are cleansed of the filth of sin. The Holy Spirit fills us. By the might of the Holy Spirit, our spirit is reborn and we are no longer bound by the laws of sin. We are then able to spend eternity with the Father in heaven.

Jesus stated that *"Flesh is born of flesh, but spirit is born of the Spirit."* John 3:6

Scriptures: Faith in Jesus

We are born again
John 3:3-6 -

Jesus replied, "Truly, truly, I tell you, no one can see the kingdom of God unless he is born again."

We are a new creation
2 Corinthians 5:17

Therefore if anyone is in Christ, he is a new creation. The old has passed away. Behold, the new has come

Romans 6:6

We know that our old self was crucified with Him so that the body of sin might be rendered powerless, that we should no longer be slaves to sin.

We are reconciled to God
2 Cor 5:18-20

All this is from God, who reconciled us to Himself through Christ and gave us the ministry of reconciliation:

that God was reconciling the world to Himself in Christ, not counting men's trespasses against them And He has committed to us the message of reconciliation.

Therefore we are ambassadors for Christ, as though God were making His appeal through us. We implore you on behalf of Christ: Be reconciled to God.

We are the Light of the world
1 Thessalonians 5:5

For you are all sons of the light and sons of the day; we do not belong to the night or to the darkness.

We are salt
Matthew 5:13
Jesus said, *"You are the salt of the earth."*

We are redeemed and adopted
Galatians 4:3-5
So also, when we were children, we were enslaved under the basic principles of the world. But when the time had fully come, God sent His Son, born of a woman, born under the law, to redeem those under the law, that we might receive our adoption as sons.

1 Peter 1:18-21
For you know that it was not with perishable things such as silver or gold that you were redeemed from the empty way of life you inherited from your forefathers, but with the precious blood of Christ, a lamb without blemish or spot.

He was known before the foundation of the world, but was revealed in the last times for your sake.

Through Him you believe in God, who raised Him from the dead and glorified Him; and so your faith and hope are in God.

We are God's children
Romans 8:14-16
For all who are led by the Spirit of God are sons of God.

For you did not receive a spirit of slavery that returns you to fear, but you received the Spirit of sonship, by whom we cry, "Abba! Father!"

The Spirit Himself testifies with our spirit that we are God's children.

John 1:12-13
But to all who did receive Him, to those who believed in His name, He gave the right to become children of God—children born not of blood, nor of the desire or will of man, but born of God.

We are joint Heirs

Galatians 4: 6-7

And because you are sons, God sent the Spirit of His Son into our hearts, crying out, "Abba, Father!" So you are no longer a slave, but a son; and since you are a son, you are also an heir through God.

Romans 8:17

And if we are children, then we are heirs: heirs of God and co-heirs with Christ—if indeed we suffer with Him, so that we may also be glorified with Him.

We are Jesus' friend

John 15:14-15 -

You are My friends if you do what I command you. No longer do I call you servants, for a servant does not understand what his master is doing. But I have called you friends, because everything I have learned from My Father I have made known to you.

We are God's workmanship

Isaiah 64:8

But now, O LORD, You are our Father, We are the clay, and You our potter; And all of us are the work of Your hand.

Psalm 100:3

Know that the LORD Himself is God; It is He who has made us, and not we ourselves; We are His people and the sheep of His pasture.

Ephesians 2:8-10

For it is by grace you have been saved through faith, and this not from yourselves; it is the gift of God, not by works, so that no one can boast.

For we are God's workmanship, created in Christ Jesus to do good works, which God prepared in advance as our way of life.

We are healed

Isaiah 53:4-5

Surely He took on our infirmities and carried our sorrows; yet we considered Him stricken by God, struck down and afflicted.

He was pierced for our transgressions, He was crushed for our iniquities; the punishment that brought us peace was upon Him, and by His stripes we are healed.

We have eternally life in Heaven
Romans 6:23

For the wages of sin is death, but the gift of God is eternal life in Christ Jesus our Lord.

Take Time to Pray, Reflect, and Write

For the word of God is living and active. Sharper than any double-edged sword, it pierces *even to dividing soul and spirit, joints and marrow. It judges the thoughts and intentions of the heart.*

Nothing in all creation is hidden from God's sight; everything is uncovered and exposed before the eyes of Him to whom we must give account. Hebrews 4:12-13

Pray about what you have read.

Reflect on the topic and scriptures provided in the section.

Write down your reflections from what you read:

- How did God's Word touch your spirit from this topic?

- In what areas did the Holy Spirit affirm God's Word in your heart?

- Did you receive a revelation from what you read? If so what?

- Is God asking you a question?

SECTION 3

PERSPECTIVE

Jesus looked at them and said, "With man this is impossible, but with God all things are possible."

Matthew 19:26

ALIVE IN CHRIST
Romans 8: 5-8

Those who live according to the flesh set their minds on the things of the flesh;

but those who live according to the Spirit set their minds on the things of the Spirit.

The mind of the flesh is death, but the mind of the Spirit is life and peace, because the mind of the flesh is hostile to God:

It does not submit to God's law, nor can it do so.

Those controlled by the flesh cannot please God.

PERSPECTIVE

D ue to our sinful nature, we now have set rules and beliefs about how things work that are in opposition to God.

It is written in Proverbs 14:12 *"There is a way which: seemeth right unto a man, but the end thereof are the ways of death."*

Our problem is that we often miss the truth that our beliefs and experiences are now based on a sinful world and a sinful nature.

In thermodynamics, one says that forward processes-pouring water from a pitcher, smoke going up a chimney, etc. are irreversible they cannot happen in reverse.

Science does not recognize the impact of sin on the world, so the idea that all real physical processes involving systems in everyday life, with many atoms or molecules are irreversible makes sense.

The accounts recorded in the Bible reveals to us that God is not bound by the laws of sin.

God states *"For my thoughts are not your thoughts, neither are your ways my ways, saith the LORD. For as the heavens are higher than the earth, so are my ways higher than your ways, and my thoughts than your thoughts."* Isaiah 55:8-9

God is holy. We are not holy. We lost our connection to Him. His mind and way of thinking are now beyond us (Psalm 77:13). God never viewed the state we are in as irreversible.

When we look at who we are and our circumstances we define it as irreversible, God does not. Grasping this concept is important, especially when we look at what is happening within our families today.

In the beginning, God also created a family structure founded on the marriage between a man and a woman united as one, but we live in a world based in sin. Like the Earth in Genesis 1:2, families are becoming a dead lifeless void without form.

Parents are killing their children. Children are killing their parents. Divorce is the new normal. A family is whatever we can bring together. Hatred, anger, and violence are becoming societal norms. For many, it seems almost impossible to resurrect anything from the emptiness felt toward each other.

God said let there be light. Jesus is the light of the world. God takes what was dead and destroyed and resurrects it into new life through Jesus.

One day Jesus was by a well *when a Samaritan woman came to draw water, Jesus said to her, "Give Me a drink." (His disciples had gone into the town to buy food.)*

"You are a Jew," said the woman. "How can You ask for a drink from me, a Samaritan woman?" (For Jews do not associate with Samaritans.)

Jesus answered, "If you knew the gift of God and who is asking you for a drink, you would have asked Him, and He would have given you living water." John 4:4-10

This woman did not know who was before her. Sin blinded her to who He really was. She saw Him through a perspective that she was unworthy to be spoken to; a person who should be stepped upon and rejected.

The woman said to Him, "Sir, give me this water so that I will not get thirsty and have to keep coming here to draw water."

Jesus told her, "Go, call your husband and come back."

"I have no husband," the woman replied.

Jesus said to her, "You are correct to say that you have no husband. In fact, you have had five husbands, and the man you now have is not your husband. You have spoken truthfully." John 4:15-18

As Jesus talked to her she experienced God's love and the perspective of who God says she is. God says she is valued; she is loved; she is delivered. All she needs to do is ask and she will be filled.

Jesus told her *".....a time is coming and has now come when the true worshipers will worship the Father in spirit and in truth, for the Father is seeking such as these to worship Him. God is Spirit and His worshipers must worship Him in spirit and in truth."*

The woman said, "I know that Messiah" (called Christ) "is coming. When He comes, He will explain everything to us."

Jesus answered, "I who speak to you am He."

Then the woman left her water jar, went back into the town, and said to the people, "Come, see a man who told me everything I ever did. Could this be the Christ?" So they left the town and made their way toward Jesus. John 4:23-26; 4:28-30

The death and resurrection of Jesus broke the laws of sin. It began the renewal process between us and God and between the old world and the new world to come

Think about what mankind originally had:

The Spirit of God was breathed into Adam.

God visited them daily.

They were unashamed in God's presence.

Their responsibilities were not difficult.

Adam and Eve were on one accord with each other.

They did not hide from God.

Sin took all of that away, but when we believe that Jesus is the Son of God we gain all of that back.

So then, just as one trespass brought condemnation for all men, so also one act of righteousness brought justification and life for all men.

For just as through the disobedience of the one man the many were made sinners, so also through the obedience of the one man the many will be made righteous. Romans 5:18-19

God does not tolerate sin (Habakkuk 1:13). He is separate from sin and He cannot be compared to us (Isaiah 40:25).

When we accept Jesus as our savior God sees us through Jesus. He says we are His children. He says we have the freedom to come before Him whenever for whatever. God says we are conquerors and in Jesus' name we have power and authority over everything. We no longer need to hide in fear but are restored to Him.

Through Christ, we are filled with the Holy Spirit. The Holy Spirit gives us the power to go against what is defined as irreversible (Zechariah 4:6). He teaches us the things of God (John 14:26). God's ways again are now able to be our ways (1 Peter 1:16).

When we look at ourselves and say I was born this way is a true statement. To say God made me this way or to say there is nothing that can change me from how I was born is not a true statement.

The Samaritan woman that Jesus met at the well was so excited about the personal experience that she had with Him that she immediately ran into the town to tell everyone to come see Him.

Many of the Samaritans from that town believed in Jesus because of the woman's testimony, "He told me everything I ever did." So when the Samaritans came to Him, they asked Him to stay with them, and He stayed two days.

And many more believed because of His message. They said to the woman, "We now believe not only because of your words; we have heard for ourselves, and we know that this man truly is the Savior of the world." John 4:39-41

When the people heard Jesus' words they asked Him to stay. They wanted to get to know Him and hear from Him. He stayed. He dwelt among them and taught them. They received Him and what He was saying. They too believed not because of the words of the woman, but because they now had a personal experience with him.

When we have a personal experience with Jesus it changes our perspective. If we choose to stay in His presence our mind is continually transformed by the power of the Holy Spirit from being carnally minded to being spiritually minded. How we view ourselves, others and life is altered. Our eyes are open and we begin to see as God sees. What was once seen as irreversible is now seen as reversible.

The Bible is filled with examples of God reversing what we define as irreversible. His actions were all a prelude to the ultimate power against the laws of sin which is the death and resurrection of Jesus.

Holy Spirit

The Holy Spirit convicts the world of sin
John 16:8-11
*But I tell you the truth, it is for your benefit that I am going away. Unless
I go away, the Advocate, will not come to you; but if I go, I will send Him
to you.*

*And when He comes, He will convict the world in regard to sin and
righteousness and judgment: in regard to sin, because they do not
believe in Me;*

*in regard to righteousness, because I am going to the Father and you
will no longer see Me; and in regard to judgment, because the prince of
this world has been condemned.*

The Holy Spirit makes believers new and gives them eternal life
Titus 3:4-7
*But when the kindness of God our Savior and His love for mankind
appeared, He saved us, not by the righteous deeds we had done, but
according to His mercy, through the washing of new birth and renewal
by the Holy Spirit.*

*This is the Spirit He poured out on us abundantly through Jesus Christ
our Savior, so that, having been justified by His grace, we would become
heirs with the hope of eternal life.*

The Holy Spirit is a seal in the lives of the believer
Ephesians 1:13-14
*And in Him, having heard and believed the word of truth—the gospel of
your salvation—you were sealed with the promised Holy Spirit, who is
the pledge of our inheritance until the redemption of those who are
God's possession, to the praise of His glory.*

The Holy Spirit dwells in believers and fills them
John 4:13-14
Jesus said to her, "Everyone who drinks this water will be thirsty again. But whoever drinks the water I give him will never thirst. Indeed, the water I give him will become in him a fount of water springing up to eternal life."

1 Corinthians 12:13
For in one Spirit we were all baptized into one body, whether Jews or Greeks, slave or free, and we were all given one Spirit to drink.

1 Corinthians 3:16-17
Do you not know that you yourselves are God's temple, and that God's Spirit dwells in you? If *anyone destroys God's temple, God will destroy him; for God's temple is holy, and you are that temple.*

The Holy Spirit is helper who teaches and reminds
John 14:26
But the Advocate, the Holy Spirit, whom the Father will send in My name, will teach you all things and will remind you of everything I have told you

1 Corinthians 2:12-13
We have not received the spirit of the world, but the Spirit who is from God, that we may understand what God has freely given us. And this is what we speak, not in words taught us by human wisdom, but in words taught by the Spirit, expressing spiritual truths in spiritual words.

The Holy Spirit is a source of revelation, wisdom, discernment, power and boldness for the believer
1 Corinthians 2:10-11
The Spirit searches all things, even the deep things of God. For who among men knows the thoughts of man except his own spirit within him? So too, no one knows the thoughts of God except the Spirit of God.

Acts 1:8
But you will receive power when the Holy Spirit comes upon you, and

you will be My witnesses in Jerusalem, and in all Judea and Samaria, and to the ends of the earth."

1 Corinthians 2:14
The natural man does not accept the things that come from the Spirit of God. For they are foolishness to him, and he cannot understand them, because they are spiritually discerned.

Acts 4:31
After they had prayed, their meeting place was shaken, and they were all filled with the Holy Spirit and spoke the word of God boldly.

The Holy Spirit guides to all truth, including knowledge of what is to come
John 16:13-15
However, when the Spirit of truth comes, He will guide you into all truth. For He will not speak on His own, but He will speak what He hears, and He will declare to you what is to come.

1 Corinthians 2:9-10
Rather, as it is written: "No eye has seen, no ear has heard, no heart has imagined, what God has prepared for those who love Him." But God has revealed it to us by the Spirit.

The Holy Spirit transforms the believer's mind and habits through sanctification
2 Thessalonians 2:13 -15
God has chosen you from the beginning to be saved by the sanctification of the Spirit and by faith in the truth. To this He called you through our gospel, so that you may share in the glory of our Lord Jesus Christ. Therefore, brothers, stand firm and cling to the traditions we taught you, whether by speech or by letter.

1 Corinthians 2:15-16
The spiritual man judges all things, but he himself is not subject to anyone's judgment. "For who has known the mind of the Lord, so as to instruct Him?" But we have the mind of Christ.

Romans 12:1-2

Therefore I urge you, brothers, on account of God's mercy, to offer your bodies as living sacrifices, holy and pleasing to God, which is your spiritual service of worship.

Do not be conformed to this world, but be transformed by the renewing of your mind. Then you will be able to test and approve what is the good, pleasing, and perfect will of God.

The Holy Spirit enables believers to bear good fruit in their lives
Galatians 5:16-18

So I say, walk by the Spirit, and you will not gratify the desires of the flesh. For the flesh craves what is contrary to the Spirit, and the Spirit what is contrary to the flesh. They are opposed to each other, so that you do not do what you want. But if you are led by the Spirit, you are not under the law.

The Holy Spirit helps in a Christian's weakness and intercedes for them
Romans 8:26-27

In the same way, the Spirit helps us in our weakness. For we do not know how we ought to pray, but the Spirit Himself intercedes for us with groans too deep for words.

And He who searches our hearts knows the mind of the Spirit, because the Spirit intercedes for the saints according to the will of God.

The Holy Spirit gives spiritual gifts to believers
1 Corinthians 12:7-11

Now to each one the manifestation of the Spirit is given for the common good.

To one there is given through the Spirit the message of wisdom, to another the message of knowledge by the same Spirit,

to another faith by the same Spirit, to another gifts of healing by that one

Spirit, to another the working of miracles, to another prophecy,

to another distinguishing between spirits, to another speaking in various tongues, and to still another the interpretation of tongues.

All these are the work of one and the same Spirit, who apportions them to each one as He determines.

Scripture: Holy Spirit Minded

Abide in Him - Bear Fruit – Love one another

John 15:5-8

I am the vine and you are the branches. The one who remains in Me, and I in him, will bear much fruit. For apart from Me you can do nothing.

If anyone does not remain in Me, he is like a branch that is thrown away and withers. Such branches are gathered up, thrown into the fire, and burned.

If you remain in Me and My words remain in you, ask whatever you wish, and it will be done for you.

This is to My Father's glory, that you bear much fruit, proving yourselves to be My disciples.

John 15:9-11

As the Father has loved Me, so have I loved you. Remain in My love.

If you keep My commandments, you will remain in My love, just as I have kept My Father's commandments and remain in His love.

I have told you these things so that My joy may be in you and your joy may be complete.

John 15: 12-13

This is My commandment, that you love one another as I have loved you. Greater love has no one than this, that he lay down his life for his friends.

John 15:16-17

You did not choose Me, but I chose you. And I appointed you to go and bear fruit—fruit that will remain—so that whatever you ask the Father in

My name, He will give you. This is My command to you: Love one another.

Be the light of the world
Matthew 5:14-16
You are the light of the world. A city on a hill cannot be hidden.

Neither do people light a lamp and put it under a basket. Instead, they set it on a stand, and it gives light to everyone in the house.

In the same way, let your light shine before men, that they may see your good deeds and glorify your Father in heaven.

Stay salty
Matthew 5:13
But if the salt loses its savor, how can it be made salty again? It is no longer good for anything, except to be thrown out and trampled by men.

Be a conqueror
Romans 8:37-39
No, in all these things we are more than conquerors through Him who loved us.

For I am convinced that neither death nor life, neither angels nor principalities, neither the present nor the future, nor any powers,

neither height nor depth, nor anything else in all creation, will be able to separate us from the love of God that is in Christ Jesus our Lord.

Trust God
Numbers 23:19
God is not a man, that He should lie, or a son of man, that He should change His mind. Does He speak and not act? Does He promise and not fulfill?

Romans 8:28
And we know that God works all things together for the good of those who love Him, who are called according to His purpose.

Jeremiah 29:11
For I know the plans I have for you, declares the LORD, plans to prosper you and not to harm you, to give you a future and a hope.

Proverbs 3:5-6
Trust in the LORD with all your heart, and lean not on your own understanding; in all your ways acknowledge Him, and He will make your paths straight.

Psalm 138:8
The LORD will accomplish what concerns me; Your loving kindness, O LORD, is everlasting;

Psalm 119:73
Your hands made me and fashioned me; Give me understanding, that I may learn Your commandments.

Matthew 10:29-31
Are not two sparrows sold for a penny? Yet not one of them will fall to the ground apart from the will of your Father.

And even the very hairs of your head are all numbered.

So do not be afraid; you are worth more than many sparrows.

Protect your mind
1 Peter 1:13
Therefore prepare your minds for action Be sober-minded. Set your hope fully on the grace to be given you at the revelation of Jesus Christ

1 Thessalonians 5:6-8
So then, let us not sleep as the others do, but let us remain awake and sober. For those who sleep, sleep at night; and those who get drunk, get drunk at night. But since we belong to the day, let us be sober, putting on the breastplate of faith and love, and the helmet of our hope of salvation.

Do not be conformed to this world
1 Peter 1:14
As obedient children, do not conform to the passions of your former ignorance.

Be Holy
1 Peter 1:15-16
But just as He who called you is holy, so be holy in all you do, for it is written: "Be holy, because I am holy."

Pull down strong holds
2 Corinthians 10:3-5
For though we live in the flesh, we do not wage war according to the flesh.

The weapons of our warfare are not the weapons of the world. Instead, they have divine power to demolish strongholds.

We tear down arguments and every presumption set up against the knowledge of God; and we take captive every thought to make it obedient to Christ.

Be Taught by the Holy Spirit
John 14:26
But the Advocate, the Holy Spirit, whom the Father will send in My name, will teach you all things and will remind you of everything I have told you.

Take Time to Pray, Reflect, and Write

For the word of God is living and active. Sharper than any double-edged sword, it **pierces** *even to dividing soul and spirit, joints and marrow. It judges the thoughts and intentions of the heart.*

Nothing in all creation is hidden from God's sight; everything is uncovered and exposed before the eyes of Him to whom we must give account. Hebrews 4:12-13

Pray about what you have read.

Reflect on the topic and scriptures provided in the section.

Write down your reflections from what you read:

- How did God's Word touch your spirit from this topic?

- In what areas did the Holy Spirit affirm God's Word in your heart?

- Did you receive a revelation from what you read? If so what?

- Is God asking you a question?

SECTION 4

DECEPTION

My son, do not forget my teaching, but let your heart keep my commandments; for they will add length to your days, years and peace to your life.

Never let loving devotion or faithfulness leave you; bind them around your neck, write them on the tablet of your heart.

Then you will find favor and high regard in the sight of God and man.

Proverbs 3:1-4

ALIVE IN CHRIST
Romans 8:9-11

You, however, are controlled not by the flesh, but by the Spirit, if the Spirit of God lives in you.

And if anyone does not have the Spirit of Christ, he does not belong to Christ.

But if Christ is in you, your body is dead because of sin,

yet your spirit is alive because of righteousness.

And if the Spirit of Him who raised Jesus from the dead is living in you,

He who raised Christ Jesus from the dead will also give life to your mortal bodies through His Spirit, who lives in you.

Therefore, brothers, we have an obligation, but it is not to the flesh, to live according to it.

For if you live according to the flesh, you will die;

but if by the Spirit you put to death the deeds of the body, you will live.

DECEPTION

The Apostle Peter wrote

"Be sober [well balanced and self-disciplined], be alert and cautious at all times. That enemy of yours, the devil, prowls around like a roaring lion [fiercely hungry], seeking someone to devour." (1 Peter 5:8 Amplified)

Satan prowls at our mind, he claws at our relationships, he devours our joy and he blocks our spiritual sight. He will pursue separating us from God and His kingdom anyway possible.

As I was studying Genesis Chapters 1-3 one of the things that caught my attention was how Eve was deceived by the serpent, which is recorded in chapter 3.

The conversation Eve had with the serpent was very mild, as is often the case with Satan. The serpent is described as being more cunning than any of the other animals in the garden (Genesis 3:1). He approaches Eve and asks the question:

"Did God really say that you must not eat of any tree in the garden?" He smoothly presents this as an innocent question.

Then Eve explains her understanding of what God has said.

"We may eat the fruit of the trees of the garden, but about the fruit of the tree in the middle of the garden, God has said, 'You must not eat of it or touch it, or you will die.'" Genesis 3:2-3

The serpent mockingly responds with the statement, *"You will not surely die."* He is leading her toward questioning the validity of God's Word.

Next, he plants the idea that God is keeping something from her that she should have.

He adds *"For God knows that in the day you eat of it, your eyes will be opened and you will be like God, knowing good and evil."* Genesis 3:5

.

Satan makes this statement in a way that presents the idea that God is purposefully not telling her the truth and God is stopping her from being equal to Him. As though being equal to God is obtainable and it is something that she deserves.

This entire situation pulls at my heart. Satan is messing with her mind and alluding to the idea of who she is now is nothing compared to who she could be or should be.

God created man. He breathed life into Adam. God created Eve from a part of Adam. They were created in the image and likeness of God.

They talked and walked with God daily and they were given authority over everything. They were perfect and already had the ultimate relationship with God

Satan's influence on our ability to believe God is huge. His sole purpose is to corrupt and destroy all that God has created that is good. He hides in the shadows so that we do not believe in his existence thus we do not see his influence upon our life.

Do not be deceived. Satan is a liar and the father of lies. Jesus said to the people.

Why do you not understand what I am saying? It is because you are unable to accept My message.

You belong to your father, the devil, and you want to carry out his desires. He was a murderer from the beginning, refusing to uphold the truth, because there is no truth in him. When he lies, he speaks his native language, because he is a liar and the father of lies.

But because I speak the truth, you do not believe Me! John 8:43-45

As Satan used the cunning skill of the serpent he uses people to deceive us. He attempts to get into our minds and twist God's word. We become convinced that what God says is not the way we should follow. This impacts our ability to believe in God and His Word.

As Jesus' time with the disciples was coming to a close He began to let them know of the difficulties ahead.

From that time on Jesus began to show His disciples that He must go to Jerusalem and suffer many things at the hands of the elders, chief priests, and scribes, and that He must be killed and on the third day be raised to life.

Peter took Him aside and began to rebuke Him. "Far be it from You, Lord!" he said. "This shall never happen to You!"

But Jesus turned and said to Peter, "Get behind Me, Satan! You are a stumbling block to Me. For you do not have in mind the things of God, but the things of men." Matthew 16:21-23

Jesus was not talking to Peter directly; He was speaking to Satan who was influencing Peter. Peter did not realize that He was going against God's plan.

Earlier Peter had been given amazing insight by the

Holy Spirit as to who Jesus is. Yet, when Jesus attempted to reveal to the disciples all that was about to happen they were not able to fully comprehend what God had ordained.

Jesus knew what the outcome would be if He was not obedient to the Father. He addressed the thought that Satan was promoting through Peter.

That thought was to pull Jesus away from His mission by getting Him to focus on Himself (the pain he was about to endure) and not on the mind of God (being the source in which all mankind can be reconciled to God if they only believe in Him.)

Satan does the same with us, which is why Paul told the Corinthians that we are not unaware of Satan's devices (2Corinthians 2:11).

He tries to lead us away from the glory that God has already given us. That glory is through faith in Jesus, our savior.

The only way to not have Satan's lies impact our belief in God's Word is to allow the Holy Spirit to lead us into all truth through God's Word.

Faith comes by hearing and hearing through the Word of God. Jesus stated, "He who has ears to hear let him hear."

Scriptures: Eyes Wide Open

Proverbs 3:7-8
Do not be wise in your own eyes; fear the LORD and turn away from evil. This will bring healing to your body and refreshment to your bones.

Matthew 24:4-5 NASB
And Jesus answered and said to them, "See to it that no one misleads you. "For many will come in My name, saying, 'I am the Christ,' and will mislead many.

Jeremiah 9:6 NASB
"Your dwelling is in the midst of deceit; Through deceit they refuse to know Me," declares the LORD.

Romans 16:17-19 NASB
Now I urge you, brethren, keep your eye on those who cause dissensions and hindrances contrary to the teaching which you learned, and turn away from them.

For such men are slaves, not of our Lord Christ but of their own appetites; and by their smooth and flattering speech they deceive the hearts of the unsuspecting.

For the report of your obedience has reached to all; therefore I am rejoicing over you, but I want you to be wise in what is good and innocent in what is evil

James 1:22
Be doers of the word, and not hearers only. Otherwise, you are deceiving yourselves.

Colossians 2:8 NASB
See to it that no one takes you captive through philosophy and empty deception, according to the tradition of men, according to the elementary principles of the world, rather than according to Christ

1 John 1:8 NASB
If we say that we have no sin, we are deceiving ourselves and the truth is not in us.

Psalm 120:1-2 NASB
In my distress I cried to the LORD, and He answered me Deliver my soul, O LORD, from lying lips and a deceitful tongue.

1 Corinthians 3:18-19 NASB
Let no man deceive himself. If any man among you thinks that he is wise in this age, he must become foolish, so that he may become wise. For the wisdom of this world is foolishness before God.

2 Corinthians 11:3-4
I am afraid, however, that just as Eve was deceived by the serpent's cunning, your minds may be led astray from your simple and pure devotion to Christ.

For if someone comes and proclaims a Jesus other than the One we proclaimed, or if you receive a different spirit than the One you received, or a different gospel than the one you accepted, you put up with it way too easily.

Hebrews 3:13-14 NASB
Take care, brethren, that there not be in any one of you an evil, unbelieving heart that falls away from the living God. But encourage one another day after day, as long as it is still called "Today," so that none of you will be hardened by the deceitfulness of sin.

1 John 3:8
The one who practices sin is of the devil, because the devil has been sinning from the very start. This is why the Son of God was revealed, to destroy the works of the devil.

John 8:44-45
You belong to your father, the devil, and you want to carry out his desires. He was a murderer from the beginning, refusing to uphold the truth, because there is no truth in him. When he lies, he speaks his native language, because he is a liar and the father of lies. But because I speak the truth, you do not believe Me!

Job 34:12
Indeed, it is true that God does not act wickedly and the Almighty does not pervert justice

1 John 1:10
If we say we have not sinned, we make Him out to be a liar, and His word is not in us.

2 Corinthians 4:6
The god of this age has blinded the minds of unbelievers so they cannot see the light of the gospel of the glory of Christ, who is the image of God.

For we do not proclaim ourselves, but Jesus Christ as Lord, and ourselves as your servants for Jesus' sake. For God, who said, "Let light shine out of darkness,"made His light shine in our hearts to give us the light of the knowledge of the glory of God in the face of Jesus Christ.

Ephesians 4:24
But this is not the way you came to know Christ.

Surely you heard of Him and were taught in Him, in keeping with the truth that is in Jesus, to put off your former way of life, your old self, which is being corrupted by its deceitful desires; to be renewed in the spirit of your minds; and to put on the new self, created to be like God in true righteousness and holiness.

Take Time to Pray, Reflect, and Write

For the word of God is living and active. Sharper than any double-edged sword, it **pierces** *even to dividing soul and spirit, joints and marrow. It judges the thoughts and intentions of the heart.*

Nothing in all creation is hidden from God's sight; everything is uncovered and exposed before the eyes of Him to whom we must give account. Hebrews 4:12-13

Pray about what you have read.

Reflect on the topic and scriptures provided in the section.

Write down your reflections from what you read:

- How did God's Word touch your spirit from this topic?

- In what areas did the Holy Spirit affirm God's Word in your heart?

- Did you receive a revelation from what you read? If so what?

- Is God asking you a question?

SECTION 5

MOCKING GOD

"I say this so that no one will delude you with persuasive argument."

Colosians 2:4 NASB

PAUL'S PRAYER
Ephesians 1:15-23

"For this reason, ever since I heard about your faith in the Lord Jesus and your love for all the saints,

I have not stopped giving thanks for you, remembering you in my prayers, in order that the God of our Lord Jesus Christ, the glorious Father, may give you a spirit of wisdom and revelation in your knowledge of Him.

I ask that the eyes of your heart may be enlightened, so that you may know the hope of His calling, the riches of His glorious inheritance in the saints,

and the surpassing greatness of His power to us who believe. These are in accordance with the working of His mighty strength,

which He exerted in Christ when He raised Him from the dead and seated Him at His right hand in the heavenly realms,

far above all rule and authority, power and dominion, and every name that is named, not only in this age, but also in the one to come.

And God put everything under His feet and made Him head over everything for the church, which is His body, the fullness of Him who fills all in all."

MOCKING GOD

We are currently living in a time in which people question God's existence and His authority regularly. Did God create heaven and earth? Did He create mankind? Did He create mankind into two distinct beings, male and female? Is His authority the only authority? Does Satan really exist? Does God still heal?

These questions and many more bombard us daily. They are frequently presented in a way that can cause us to doubt God and lose faith in the Biblical truths of the Bible.

We start to take the Bible and the Word of God as just a book with some interesting stories. Jesus becomes a footnote that references a nice guy who simply said we should love one another.

Asking God a question is not a horrible thing, but questioning is wrong when it is used as a disguise to mock God.

Satan mocks God's Word. God's Word is a reflection of Himself. The Bible tells us, *The Word became flesh and made His dwelling among us. We have seen His glory, the glory of the one and only Son from the Father, full of grace and truth* John 1:14

Jesus is God's Word in the flesh. God's Word reveals His character, nature, love, plan for mankind, and how we should live our life.

Jesus stated, *Do you not believe that I am in the Father and the Father is in Me? The words I say to you, I do not speak on My own. Instead, it is the Father dwelling in Me, performing His works. Believe Me that I am in the Father and the Father is in Me—or at least believe on account of the works themselves.* John 14:10-11

Mocking God is when we doubt or nullify God's Word as though it is not the truth. In other words, we do not believe God is who He says He is and we do not believe He will do what He says He will do.

Satan knows that our thoughts direct our beliefs and our beliefs direct our actions.

For those that are saved by faith in Jesus Christ, Satan mock's God as a means to:

- get us to leave the position of authority which God has already given us.
-
- convince us that God is a liar, a deceiver and is withholding real blessings from us.

- deceive us into believing that what he is offering is better than what God has given us.

- confuse our minds and have us fall away from the truths of God's Word.

The Holy Spirit tells us, *Do not be deceived: God is not to be mocked. Whatever a man sows, he will reap in returs. The one who sows to please his flesh, from the flesh will reap destruction; but the one who sows to please the Spirit, from the Spirit will reap eternal life.* Galatians 6:7

Sowing to the flesh is following our own desires. Doing things the way we want too not the way God has ordain and His Spirit leads us to do them. It is impossible to please God when flesh guides our life.

Sowing to the Spirit is when we seek to be led by the Holy Spirit and do the will of God.

Jesus experienced Satan's mocking on multiple occasions when he was on earth. One of these moments occurred just after he had His position as the son of God affirmed by God.

As soon as Jesus was baptized, He went up out of the water. Suddenly the heavens were opened, and He saw the Spirit of God descending like a dove and resting on Him. And a voice from heaven said, "This is My beloved Son, in whom I am well pleased! Matthew 3:16-17

Then Jesus was led by the Spirit into the wilderness to be tempted by the devil. After fasting forty days and forty nights, He was hungry.

The tempter came to Him and said, "If You are the Son of God, tell these stones to become bread."

But Jesus answered, "It is written:' Man shall not live on bread alone, but on every word that comes from the mouth of God.'"

Then the devil took Him to the holy city and set Him on the pinnacle of the temple. "If You are the Son of God," he said, "throw Yourself down. For it is written: He will command His angels concerning You, and they will lift You up in their hands, so that You will not strike Your foot against a stone.' "

Jesus replied, "It is also written: 'Do not put the Lord your God to the test.' "

Again, the devil took Him to a very high mountain and showed Him all the kingdoms of the world and their glory." All this I will give You," he said, "if You will fall down and worship me."

"Away from Me, Satan!" Jesus declared. "For it is written: 'Worship the Lord your God and serve Him only.' "

Then the devil left Him, and angels came and ministered to Him
Matthew 4:1-11

When Jesus was fasting, each time Satan came to Him, He quoted God's Word and stood on it. He did not add to it nor did he consider what Satan was presenting as desirable over obeying God.

Eve was deceived into thinking eating the fruit, although it disobeyed God, was a good way to gain wisdom.

When the woman saw that the tree was good for food and pleasing to the eyes, and that it was desirable for obtaining wisdom, she took the fruit and ate it. Genesis 3:6

We are being deceived and entertaining a mocking spirit against God when:

- equality with God is promoted and His Sovereignty (God's supreme power and authority) is rejected.

- the validity of God's Word is questioned as a means to prove God is not who He says He is.

- When God's Word is intentionally distorted and manipulated away from the truth.

In order to not be deceived we need to learn to discern when God is being mocked. The only way to do this is to know God and His Word through faith in Jesus Christ by the leading of the Holy Spirit.

Scriptures: Our Sword

God's Word

John 1:1
In the beginning was the Word, and the Word was with God, and the Word was God.

Psalm 119:160
The entirety of Your word is truth, and all Your righteous judgments endure forever

Isaiah 40:8
The grass withers and the flowers fall, but the word of our God stands forever."

Hebrews 4:12
For the word of God is living and active. Sharper than any double-edged sword, it pierces even to dividing soul and spirit, joints and marrow. It judges the thoughts and intentions of the heart.

John 6:66-69
From that time on many of His disciples turned back and no longer walked with Him. So Jesus asked the Twelve, "Do you want to leave too?" Simon Peter replied, "Lord, to whom would we go? You have the words of eternal life. We believe and know that You are the Holy One of God."

Isaiah 55:11
so My word that proceeds from My mouth will not return to Me empty, but it will accomplish what I please, and it will prosper where I send it.

1 Corinthians 1:18
For the message of the cross is foolishness to those who are perishing, but to us who are being saved it is the power of God

Isaiah 29:13-14
Therefore I will again confound these people with wonder upon wonder. The wisdom of the wise will vanish, and the intelligence of the intelligent will be hidden.

1 Corinthians 1:20
Where is the wise man? Where is the scribe? Where is the philosopher of this age? Has not God made foolish the wisdom of the world?

1 Corinthians 21
For since in the wisdom of God the world through its wisdom did not know Him, God was pleased through the foolishness of what was preached to save those who believe.

Romans 1:17
For the gospel reveals the righteousness of God that comes by faith from start to finish ,just as it is written: "The righteous will live by faith."

Deuteronomy 8:3
man does not live on bread alone, but on every word that comes from the mouth of the LORD.

John 16:13-15
However, when the Spirit of truth comes, He will guide you into all truth. For He will not speak on His own, but He will speak what He hears, and He will declare to you what is to come.

John 14:26
But the Advocate, the Holy Spirit, whom the Father will send in My name, will teach you all things and will remind you of everything I have told you.

Psalm 119:105
Your word is a lamp to my feet and a light to my path.

Obedience to God's Word

Exodus 19:5
Now if you will indeed obey My voice and keep My covenant, you will be My treasured possession out of all the nations—for the whole earth is Mine.

Jeremiah 7:3
Thus says the LORD of Hosts, the God of Israel: Correct your ways and your deeds, and I will let you live in this place.

Romans 1:5-6
Through Him and on behalf of His name, we received grace and apostleship to call all those among the Gentiles to the obedience that comes from faith. And you also are among those who are called to belong to Jesus Christ.

Romans 6:17-18
But thanks be to God that, though you once were slaves to sin, you wholeheartedly obeyed the form of teaching to which you were committed. You have been set free from sin and have become slaves to righteousness.

Romans 10:16-16-17
For Isaiah says, "Lord, who has believed our message?" Consequently, faith comes by hearing, and hearing by the word of Christ.

1 Samuel15:22
"Does the LORD delight in burnt offerings and sacrifices as much as in obedience to His voice? Behold, obedience is better than sacrifice, and attentiveness is better than the fat of rams.

1 Samuel 15:23
For rebellion is like the sin of divination, and arrogance is like the wickedness of idolatry

Because you have rejected the word of the LORD, He has rejected you as king."

Jeremiah 26:13

So now, correct your ways and deeds, and obey the voice of the LORD your God, so that He might relent of the disaster He has pronounced against you.

Deuteronomy 11:13

So if you carefully obey the commandments I am giving you today, to love the LORD your God and to serve Him with all your heart and with all your soul,

then I will provide rain for your land in season, the autumn and spring rains, that you may gather your grain, new wine, and oil. And I will provide grass in the fields for your livestock, and you will eat and be satisfied.

Jeremiah 38:20

"They will not hand you over," Jeremiah replied. "Obey the voice of the LORD in what I am telling you, that it may go well with you and you may live.

Isaiah 1:19

If you are willing and obedient, you will eat the best of the land. But if you resist and rebel, you will be devoured by the sword."

James 1:23

But the one who looks intently into the perfect law of freedom, and continues to do so—not being a forgetful hearer, but an effective doer— he will be blessed in what he does.

Deuteronomy 28:13

The LORD will make you the head and not the tail; you will only move upward and never downward, if you hear and carefully follow the commandments of the LORD your God, which I am giving you today.

Do not turn aside to the right or to the left from any of the words I command you today, and do not go after other gods to serve them.

John 15:10

If you keep My commandments, you will remain in My love, just as I have kept My Father's commandments and remain in His love.

1 Peter 1:14-16
As obedient children, do not conform to the passions of your former ignorance. But just as He who called you is holy, so be holy in all you do, or it is written: "Be holy, because I am holy.

Romans 2:13
For it is not the hearers of the law who are righteous before God, but it is the doers of the law who will be declared righteous.

Romans 2:6-8
God "will repay each one according to his deeds."

To those who by perseverance in doing good seek glory, honor, and immortality, He will give eternal life.

But for those who are self-seeking and who reject the truth and follow wickedness, there will be wrath and anger.

Take Time to Pray, Reflect, and Write

For the word of God is living and active. Sharper than any double-edged sword, it **pierces** *even to dividing soul and spirit, joints and marrow. It judges the thoughts and intentions of the heart.*

Nothing in all creation is hidden from God's sight; everything is uncovered and exposed before the eyes of Him to whom we must give account. Hebrews 4:12-13

Pray about what you have read.

Reflect on the topic and scriptures provided in the section.

Write down your reflections from what you read:

- How did God's Word touch your spirit from this topic?

- In what areas did the Holy Spirit affirm God's Word in your heart?

- Did you receive a revelation from what you read? If so what?

- Is God asking you a question?

STEPS TO ALIGN WITH GOD

Now we see but a dim reflection as in a mirror; then we shall see face to face. Now I know in part; then I shall know fully, even as I am fully known.

1 Corinthians 13:12

WHOLE ARMOR OF GOD
Ephesians 6:10-20

Finally, be strong in the Lord and in His mighty power. Put on the full armor of God, so that you can make your stand against the devil's schemes.

For our struggle is not against flesh and blood, but against the rulers, against the authorities, against the powers of this world's darkness, and against the spiritual forces of evil in the heavenly realms.

Therefore take up the full armor of God, so that when the day of evil comes, you will be able to stand your ground, and having done everything, to stand.

Stand firm then, with the belt of truth buckled around your waist, with the breastplate of righteousness arrayed, and with your feet fitted with the readiness of the gospel of peace.

In addition to all this, take up the shield of faith, with which you can extinguish all the flaming arrows of the evil one.

And take the helmet of salvation and the sword of the Spirit, which is the word of God.

Pray in the Spirit at all times, with every kind of prayer and petition. To this end, stay alert with all perseverance in your prayers for all the saints.

Pray also for me (pastors, ministers, priest, missionaries, evangelist, teachers of the gospel), that whenever I (they) open my (their) mouth, divine utterance may be given me (them),

so that I (they) will boldly make known the mystery of the gospel, for which I am (they are) an ambassador in chains.

Pray that I (they) may proclaim it fearlessly, as I (they) should.

Take Time to Read, Reflect, and Write

The goal of our instruction is the love that comes from a pure heart, a clear conscience, and a sincere faith.

Some have strayed from these ways and turned aside to empty talk.

They want to be teachers of the law, but they do not understand what they are saying or that which they so confidently assert. 1Timothy 1:5-7

- Choose to do a personal study of the referenced chapters and books of the Bible.

  Genesis Chapters 1-3

  The Gospels

  Book of Acts

  Romans

- Write down the thoughts, insight and questions that come to mind as you read.

- Set a place and time to read.

- Take your time when reading and reread the same chapter multiple times.

Take Time to Pray

If you remain in me and my words remain in you ask whatever you wish and it will be done for you. John 15:7

Write your own prayers. Search God's Word for scripture or use the ones referenced throughout the book to help guide you.

- Ask the Holy Spirit to guide you as you read.

- Pray for the Holy Spirit to give you understanding about what you are reading.

- Pray for the Holy Spirit to help you to surrender to His truth.

- Connect your prayers to the reflections from your reading of the topics or the Bible.

Prayer, Praise and Thanks

- Heavenly Father, You are Lord and creator of all. I thank You and praise You for Your loving devotion and Your faithfulness.

- Fill me Holy Spirit that Your Word is a lamp to my feet and a light to guide my path.

- Jesus you are the author and finisher of my faith. Strengthen me so I do not turn away from the truth of Your Word.

- Lord when I lean on my own understanding it opens the door for me to be deceived. Please give me a spirit of discernment that I may see the snares of Satan.

- Jesus you are my Lord and Savior in You do I trust!

- My Holy Father, "Who is like You among the gods, O LORD? Who is like You, majestic in holiness, Awesome in praises, working wonders?" I give thanks to you Lord for all of your works.

- Jesus you have sole authority. You have the final say in my life. Whatever I think I see, no matter what someone says or claims about me it doesn't matter. You are my healer, you are my protector, you are my deliverer. I thank you and praise you my King!

- Thank you God for Your Indescribable Gift! Your Holy Servant! Your One Who Sets Me Free!!

- Lord, I pray that you will open the eyes of believers and give us hearts of love and compassion for the lost.

- Holy Spirit, fill _____ that _____ may know you. Help _____ to stand upon Your Word and learn each precept as Your Spirit leads. (refer to yourself or another)

- Lord, I pray for the heart of _____ that Your Spirit will fill _____ completely with joy and grace. (refer to yourself or another)

- You know and see _____ struggles, deliver and meet _____ in the secret places of _____ heart. (refer to yourself or another)

- Shape and correct _____ thoughts, words, and actions that are not of you. Create in _____ a clean heart. (refer to yourself or another)

- Lord answer _____ prayers according to Your will and glory. So, that you will be glorified in _____ life and _____ faith will be fortified. (refer to yourself or another)

- Holy Spirit I pray that You help _____ to learn to abide in You, be filled with Your Spirit, and live according to Your will. I pray this for _____, _____ family, _____ church, the Church, and _____ community. (refer to yourself or another)

- Lord, I pray that _____ will walk in love, kindness, mercy and grace with the lost and other believers. (refer to yourself or another)

- Holy Spirit provide _____ with insight and wisdom into each situation of _____ day. (refer to yourself or another).

In Jesus' Name

Almighty One – *"...who is and who was and who is to come, the Almighty."* Revelations 1:8

Alpha and Omega – *"I am the Alpha and the Omega, the First and the Last, the Beginning and the End."* Revelations 22:13

Advocate – *"My dear children, I write this to you so that you will not sin. But if anybody does sin, we have an advocate with the Father--Jesus Christ, the Righteous One."* 1 John 2:1

Author and Perfecter of my Faith – *"Fixing our eyes on Jesus, the author and perfecter of faith, who for the joy set before Him endured the cross, despising the shame, and has sat down at the right hand of the throne of God."* Hebrews 12:2

Authority – *"Jesus said, 'All authority in heaven and on earth has been given to me."* Matthew 28:18

Bread of Life – *"Then Jesus declared, 'I am the bread of life. Whoever comes to me will never go hungry, and whoever believes in me will never be thirsty.'"* John 6:35

Beloved Son of God – *"And behold, a voice from heaven said, "This is my beloved Son, with whom I am well pleased."* Matthew 3:17

Bridegroom – *"And Jesus said to them, "Can the wedding guests mourn as long as the bridegroom is with them? The days will come when the bridegroom is taken away from them, and then they will fast."* Matthew 9:15

Chief Cornerstone – *"The stone which the builders rejected has become the chief corner stone."* Psalm 118:22

Deliverer – *"And to wait for his Son from heaven, whom he raised from the dead, Jesus who delivers us from the wrath to come."* 1 Thessalonians 1:10

Faithful and True – *"I saw heaven standing open and there before me was a white horse, whose rider is called Faithful and True. With justice he judges and wages war."* Revelations 19:11

Good Shepherd - *"I am the good shepherd. The good shepherd lays down his life for the sheep."* John 10:11

Great High Priest – *"Therefore, since we have a great high priest who has passed through the heavens, Jesus the Son of God, let us hold fast our confession."* Hebrews 4:14

Head of the Church – *"And he put all things under his feet and gave him as head over all things to the church."* Ephesians 1:22

Holy Servant – *"...and grant that Your bond-servants may speak Your word with all confidence, while You extend Your hand to heal, and signs and wonders take place through the name of Your holy servant Jesus."* Acts 4:29-30

I Am – *"Jesus said to them, "Truly, truly, I say to you, before Abraham was, I am."* John 8:58

Immanuel – *"...She will give birth to a son and will call him Immanuel, which means 'God with us.'"* Isaiah 7:14

Indescribable Gift – *"Thanks be to God for His indescribable gift."* 2 Corinthians 9:15

Judge – *"...he is the one whom God appointed as judge of the living and the dead."* Acts 10:42

King of Kings – *"These will wage war against the Lamb, and the Lamb will overcome them, because He is Lord of lords and King of kings, and those who are with Him are the called and chosen and faithful."* Revelations 17:14

Lamb of God – *"The next day John saw Jesus coming toward him and said, "Look, the Lamb of God, who* takes away the sin of the world!" John 1:29

Light of the World – *"I am the light of the world. Whoever follows me will never walk in darkness, but will have the light of life."* John 8:12

Lion of the Tribe of Judah – *"Weep no more; behold, the Lion of the tribe of Judah, the Root of David, has conquered, so that he can open the scroll and its seven seals."* Revelations 5:5

Jesus You are Lord of All – *"For this reason also, God highly exalted Him, and bestowed on Him the name which is above every name, so that at the name of Jesus every knee will bow, of those who are in heaven and on earth and under the earth, and that every tongue will confess that Jesus Christ is Lord, to the glory of God the Father."* Philippians 2:9-11

Jesus You are my Mediator – *"For there is one God, and one mediator between God and men, the man Christ Jesus."* 1 Timothy 2:5

Messiah – *"We have found the Messiah" (that is, the Christ)."* John 1:41

Mighty One – *"Then you will know that I, the Lord, am your Savior, your Redeemer, the Mighty One of Jacob."* Isaiah 60:16

One Who Sets me Free – *"So if the Son sets you free, you will be free indeed."* John *8:36*

Hope – *"...Christ Jesus our hope."* 1 Timothy 1:1

Peace – *"For he himself is our peace, who has made the two groups one and has destroyed the barrier, the dividing wall of hostility,"* Ephesians 2:14

Father's Prophet – *"And Jesus said to them, "A prophet is not without honor, except in his hometown and among his relatives and in his own household."* Mark 6:4

Redeemer – *"And as for me, I know that my Redeemer lives, and at the last He will take His stand on the earth."* Job 19:25

Risen Lord – *"...that Christ died for our sins according to the Scriptures, that he was buried, that he was raised on the third day according to the Scriptures."* 1Corinthians15:3-4

Rock – *"For they drank from the spiritual Rock that followed them, and the Rock was Christ."* 1 Corinthians10:4

Sacrifice for my Sins – *"This is love: not that we loved God, but that he loved us and sent his Son as an atoning sacrifice for our sins."* 1 John 4:10

Savior – *"For unto you is born this day in the city of David a Savior, who is Christ the Lord."* Luke 2:11

Son of Man – *"For the Son of Man came to seek and to save the lost."* Luke 19:10

Son of the Most High – *"He will be great and will be called the Son of the Most High. The Lord God will give him the throne of his father David."* Luke 1:32

Supreme Creator Over All – *"By Him all things were created, both in the heavens and on earth, visible and invisible, whether thrones or dominions or rulers or authorities-- all things have been created through Him and for Him. He is before all things, and in Him all things hold together...."* Colossians1:16-17

Resurrection and the Life – *"Jesus said to her, "I am the resurrection and the life. The one who believes in me will live, even though they die."* John 11:25

The Door – *"I am the door. If anyone enters by me, he will be saved and will go in and out and find pasture."* John 10:9

The Way – *"Jesus answered, "I am the way and the truth and the life. No one comes to the Father except through me."* John 14:6

The Word – *"In the beginning was the Word, and the Word was with God, and the Word was God."* John 1:1

True Vine - *"I am the true vine, and My Father is the vinedresser."* John 15:1

Truth – *"And you will know the truth, and the truth will set you free."* John 8:32

Victorious One – *"To the one who is victorious, I will give the right to sit with me on my throne, just as I was victorious and sat down with my Father on his throne."* Revelations 3:21

Wonderful Counselor, Mighty God, Everlasting Father, Prince of Peace – *"For to us a child is born, to us a son is given, and the government will be on his shoulders. And he will be called Wonderful Counselor, Mighty God, Everlasting Father, Prince of Peace."* Isaiah 9:6

ABOUT THE AUTHOR

Crystal Hood is a born again Christian who has been a servant of the Lord for more than four decades. She began writing about her life, family, and spiritual journey on a request from a friend in March 2010. To her surprise and joy, the Lord used her writing to minister to herself and others. Over the years she has published approximately thirty-five articles, nine poems, and three books.

Aligning Yourself with God Series:

When Joy Speaks

How You Choose to Respond to God

The Sin Crouching at Your Door